THE WORLD

OF

HACKING

BY: PARTH GOYAL

DISCLAIMER

ALL THE INFORMATION PROVIDED IN THIS BOOK IS ONLY FOR EDUCATIONAL PURPOSES. NO PARTH OF THIS BOOK MAY NOT BE REPRODUCED IN ANY FROM WITHOUT THE PRIOR PERMISSION FROM ME OWNER OF THE BOOK AND I AM NOT TAKE ANY LEGAL RESPONSINILITY FOR ANY ERROR OR MISREPRESENTATATIONS THAT MAY HAVE CREPT IN. I HAVE TRIED MY BEEST EFFORTS TO PROVIDE ACCURATE INFORMATION IN THIS BOOK. ALL THE CONTENT AND IMAGES YOU IN THIS BOOK ARE FROM INTERNET RESEARCH AND ON MY OPNION. SO BEFORE FOLLOWING ANY PART OF THE BOOK PLEASE LEARN MORE ABOUT THE TOPIC.

CHAPTERS-

1. TYPES OF HACKER

2. WAYS OF HACKING

3. WHY TO LEARN BASIC HACKING IS IMPORTANT

4. SCOPE OF HACKING IN THE WORLD OF INTERNET

5. PROTECTION AGAINST SOCIAL ATTACK

TYPES OF HACKER'S

There are many types of hacker but mainly we can classify them into three main categories. This are-

1. White Hat Hacker

2. Gray Hat Hacker

3. Black Hat Hacker

So let's understand each of them in more detail

1. White Hat Hacker

The term '**White Hat**' refers to '**Ethical Hackers** or **Computer Security Expert** '.

Basically white hat hackers are those hackers which use their skills to check and improve the security by fixing the vulnerabilities in a system. They use their skills for the benefits of the society or for the organizations. The white hat hackers are hired by the business/organization/company to check there system security to protect from hack. The white hat hacker first take the proper permission from the owner of the company and legally try to hack there system and find vulnerabilities if they hack there system or found any vulnerabilities in there system they fix it and get paid very good amount of money for their work (we will talk more about scope of white hat hacker in chapter 4) and we also know these hacker as a **'Good Hacker'** with good intention because they never violate laws of ethical hacking.

2. Gray Hat Hacker

A **'Gray Hat'** is a type of hacker or security expert who may sometimes **violate laws of ethical hacking but with good intension or just for their fun.** These hacker hack the system without the permission of the business, company or organizations but after hacking or after finding the vulnerabilities in the system of that business or organizations or they also work for the public welfare if the company or business going wrong they leak there data to public but it is illegal according to the laws of ethical hacking and against these people (hacker) the organization, business or company can file report against them and the hacker will be jailed. These hacker many also hack the system for their fun not to harm them and they never use data for illegal purposes. The intension of grey hat hacker is not to violate the rules and regulation or to disturb the service of the organization, company or business and they did not leak there data or did not use their data for own benefits.

But according to the rules of ethical hacking the gray hat hacker are violate their rules so they may be to face jail for their illogical work.

NOTE-**So before hacking any system always take proper permission form that organization, business or company**.

3. Black Hat Hacker

IMPORTANT-**IT IS ILLEGICAL AND YOU WILL BE JAILED IF YOU DO BLACK HAT HACKING**.

Black Hat hackers are those hackers who hack the system for their personal gain or maliciousness like they can hack your social media account or bank account etc and use for illegal purposes.

IN CHAPTER 5 WE WILL TALK MORE ABOUT BASIC STEPS TO PROTECT FROM BLACK HAT HACKERS.

CHAPTER- 1 COMPLETED

I HOPE YOU LEARN SOMETHING NEW SO NOW IT'S TIME TO GO ON OUR NEW CHAPTER

WAYS TO HACKING

There are many ways to hack a system and hacker also tried to find a new ways to hack you. In this chapter we are going to understand some basic ways to hack

1. **Phishing**

   Phishing is the attempt to acquire sensitive information such as your username, password, your credit card details and many more.

   Phishing itself a big topic and in phishing there are many ways to hack so let's first understand the meaning of phishing.

   In phishing the hacker create a fake web page/ login page or a website which look like original page and somehow convince you to login on these fake website pages By sending fake offers, promises or any other eye catching things.

   This can be done by the means of SMS, MMS,

and On Social Networking Sites. When you open these fake web page or website (in chapter-5 we will understand how can you differentiate between real and fake website or web page) it look similar to original page and some time it is difficult to differentiate between real and a fake website page and it ask you to enter details login or excess the website when you enter your details to that page these details where store in the hacker server and you will hacked. (In last chapter we will understand how to differentiate between real and fake web page). By this method many criminal minded peoples are stealing information from common peoples who does not have a proper knowledge of cyber tricks and hacking.

So let's now we are going to understand the mechanism of phishing and how it works. We already know about how this fake website or pages are created and we also know about how hackers take you on these website or pages (methods) and take your information. Now the question arises what happen after entering your personal details.

So when you enter your personal details and click on login button all the data throw internet all the data stored in hacker's server and now the data is now in control of hacker and now the website is coded like that it will automatically transfer or redirect to you on original website and a normal people things that it is a normal error and he/she forgot it but your personal data is now in the control of hacker and the hacker can use their data for illegal purposes and it gives you a great loss. These types of fake web pages are created throw coding and uploading to private server so it create a barrier or create difficulty to track the hacker by police but it is not impossible and police will tracked you by many method.

Image of face book fake page and a real page and we will discuss more in chapter-5

NOTE-Phishing is illegal, and by this method many criminal minded peoples are stealing information from common peoples who does not have a proper knowledge of cyber tricks and hacking.

IN CHAPTER-5 WE WILL BASICALLY UNDERSTAND HOW CAN YOU CHECK THE PAGE IS REAL OR NOT BY JUST SOME SIMPLE STEPS.

2. **Key logger-**

    Key logger is a type of surveillance software (considered to be either software or spyware that has the capability to record every key which you type by the help of your physical keyboard or by the help of inbuilt keyboard (like as in your mobile phone or laptop)) and makes a log file which is usually encrypted and it record instant messages, e-mail or any other information you type with the help of your keyboard.

So whenever you enter anything on your computer with the help of your keyboard (both) it will secretly stores in key logger.

There are two types of key loggers

a) **Software key logger** – This key logger are install in your computer or hidden in a computer and whenever you type in your computer they store in encrypted file without the permission of the owner. This software in not easily detectable by normal person. So all the data which you are typed with the help of keyword are after readable and your personal data may be used for illegal purposes.

Software key logger Basically of two types	
Those which are install by the owner of the system.	Those which install with other software or by any other way and sends your data throw internet to their internet

They did not need internet for their work.	They need internet for their work.

b) **Physical key logger** – This type of key logger are seen is mostly public computers like cyber café. The hardware or physical key logger is attached to the system and whenever you type in this system they where store in key logger and after this details are further used by the owner of cyber café.

Types of data key logger store-

everything which you type with the help of key logger are stored in the key logger like your bank account details, card details , personal chat, personal data etc.

How to protect from key logger-

always evade/escape entering personal information in public computer and before using the computer check, if you find any key logger then complain against the cyber café owner.

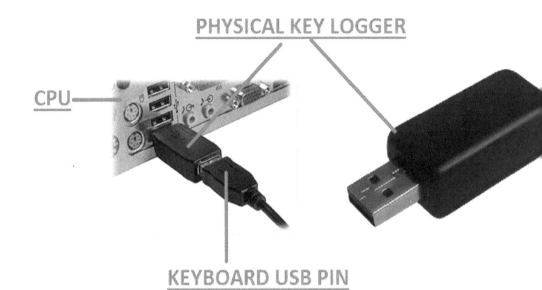

The above image of key logger helps you to find easily if they are present in computer

3. Man In The Middle Attack

According to his name says '**Man in the middle**' a hacker attack on their victim by intercepting the victim's communication.

Let's understand this with an example-

You are using internet throw Wi-Fi so all the data which you sends or revives go throw the Wi-Fi if a person (hacker) intercept your communications between your server and the device(the data which you are sending or receiving throw internet) so that they can excess your communications and also do changes with it.

These types of attack are mainly done on those Wi-Fi routers which have poor quality of security. Those people who use public Wi-Fi have more change to be hacked so didn't use open public Wi-Fi until you are not sour with them.

4. **Malware Attack**

Malware is an abbreviated form of '**malicious software'.** These types of software are specially coded to access the data of the victim's device. These types of software are downloaded with the files without the permission of the owner of that device basically for their personal profit of the hacker. This are download with other software which is already affected by this malware.

This type of malware can attack in all type of devices like windows, android, macOS and IOS.

This type of malware are mostly download from those software which are unauthorized or not download throw play store (android) and app store (IOS).

To protect from these malware attack always try to download application for respective app store but something the app store application may also be affect with malware but it is the safe and easiest way to protect themselves from malware free software.

Note- malware mainly downloaded when you try to download pirated content like games, movies, software etc or visit websites like porn websites, when you install this software they may also install and store in your system.

Types of malwares- Viruses, spyware (for stealing sensitive information), ransom ware, adware (for forced advertising to earn profits), Trojan horses, zombie computers (for email spam) and many other types.

So let's now understand more about spyware and how its work-

Spyware-It is type of software, command line or a program which stolen data (personal details like as your password, credit card, personal image or any other data) from your pc mobile and computer and sends this data to their owner (hacker). These type of malware (spyware) are mainly downloaded in your pc which you download anything from the internet,

Basically it is mainly seen that when you try to download pirated content like movies, games, software etc from internet this small spyware is also downloaded with them because a software has thousands of file to install them and this spyware is attach with and download in your system and normal people cannot detect them and when you install this software they also install in your system(in the files so it can't be detectable easily) and when you connect to the internet this spyware start their function and sends personal data like your bank details which you enter earlier for online payment and also sends your personal other data to their owner and many times the owner of spyware leak this data and it gives great loss to the people and if the spyware install in the system of organization/business/company it may lead to great damage for the organization/company/business because in the today's world maximum of the data of the organization/business/company are stored in her system or internet server.

Now in chapter-5 we will understand how you can protect yourself or your organization form these spyware.

Note- if you are using the system of your organization or your personal computer where your personal data is stored then try to avoid to download unwanted files from internet and use good anti-virus to protect the system.

5. Denial of service attack(DDOS ATTACK)

Basically denial of service attack (**Dos** or **Ddos** attack) is a type of cyber attack in which the victim website is flooded with traffic of fake users created by the hacker to make slow down there website or makes temporary unavailable for the real user of the website, it create a great loss to the website owner.

Let's now understand in some more details with example

Let's suppose you are an website owner where you are selling clothes for mans and women's and you are on the best seller and any other person who also want to start same business and want to sell clothes online but you are the best seller so why people visit on their website to buy clothes. So the people make do **dos** attack or hire black hat hacker to perform dos attack on their website and makes your website temporary unavailable for their buyers and then by using marketing he/she can attract there buyers on your website and earn profit from it.

Now the question arises what is the benefits of hacker and how this attack perform

So first we will understand how dos attack perform

The hacker sends fake users on the victim website which lead to more traffic on their website and as we know that every website has limit (e.g. how many people visit website in per second) let's suppose your website can handle 100 people per second but the hacker sends suppose 150 or 200 users per second.

Note – before performing the **dos** attack the hacker that complete information regards your website like who is the owner of the company website, there address, your server address , limit and many other required things before to hack the website.

It is because denial of service is illegal and criminal offence.

After getting all the information the hacker perform dos attack on victim website which lead to more traffic and the website will become temporary down or not respond here the hacker work will complete after this attack real user of the website which are buying product from the website are unable to buy which lead to great loss to the owner of the website and the competitor can attract there audience or buyers to their website.

Now let's understand what are benefits of dos attack to the hacker

Basically the hacker didn't have any profit from them but it leads damage to the owner of the website. This attack is mostly used to anxious or for the revenge to the owner of the website and the hacker will be jailed because **ddos** attack in term of ethical hacking.

WARNING: - ALL the ways are illegal and you will be jailed if you are for illegal purposes. So before using this ways please take proper and complete permission with the owner of the company, organization or where as you are using these ways or any other ways of hacking. All the ways are only for educational purposes and to protect themselves or to help the people

In chapter-5 we will understand basically how can you protect yourself from these types of hacking attacks or protect your organization and help them. (Only use them as educational purpose and to protect themselves)

Chapter-2 completed

I HOPE YOU LEARN SOMETHING NEW SO NOW IT'S TIME TO GO ON OUR NEW CHAPTER.

WHY TO LEARN BASIC HACKING IS IMPORTANT

In the today's growing world of internet millions of people come online daily and serve internet and also many companies are also on internet to sell their service or product online but with the growing of internet the social crime is also growing with internet and hacker also try different methods to hack you to stolen your personal details like your bank details social media account or many other personal details which affect your life.

Growing internet also lead to growing crime but in chapter-2 we already understand some of the basic ways to hack a system and in chapter-5 we will understand some ways so you can protect yourself or your business or organization from this social attacks and by using this basic ways you can protect yourself these attacks. But in this chapter we will understand **why to learn basic hacking is important and there benefits.**

By learning some basic steps of hacking you may protect yourself from stolen your-

- **Bank details**
- **Personal details**
- **Personal chat**
- **Card details**
- **Business data and many others.**

In the growing world of online business they needs to protect their data also from hackers so these organization business or company hire cyber security hacker (white hat hacker- already explain in chapter-1) to check the vulnerabilities or security of the system and they paid a very good amount of money and this is also one of the most reputed work in the field of internet and it also give opportunities to many people to make carrier in this field.

In the growing demand of internet the demand of this hackers(white hat) also increases with time and in chapter-4 we will understand more about this topic and how can you will become cyber security expert(this field also did not required any degree it just need how can you protect and help the society-discus all these things in chapter-4)

Chapter-3 completed

I HOPE YOU LEARN SOMETHING NEW SO NOW IT'S TIME TO GO ON OUR NEW CHAPTER.

SCOPE OF HACKING IN THE WORLD OF INTERNET

In chapter-1 we already talk about how white hat hacker protect the system of the company, business or organization from hacking for their good work these hackers are also know as good hackers.

As we know all the companies are now coming online to sell their product or services from digital medium. Digital service is also growing with time daily 'millions' of people use internet to transfers money or to buy something online or to buy products or services online and many companies depends on internet for their business but black hat hacker (already discussed in chapter-1 who is black hat hacker) use internet in different ways to hack (some ways of hacking is already disused in chapter-2) so to protect the companies or organizations. The white hat hacker are hired by the business to check the vulnerabilities in there system because now these dates many important data or the business are stored in there system or on the internet.

Let's take an example for better understanding

- Now maximum of the banks are now online and millions of people excess there bank account online and transfer money (digital money) from one account to another or for digital/online payment. If any of these bank website will hacked them it will create a great loss of money and the users of the bank get disturbed and they did not access their money or use their money because all the money of the bank are under control in the hacker and it also create great loss of money.

  So to protect these website , the bank or business/ organization/companies hire 'white hat hackers' to protect their system from 'black hat hacker' and time to time they will update their security so no one can hack there system and they can protected from social attacks.

Now many 'white hat hacker' works for a particular companies/ business/ organizations because 'black hat hacker' always try to find new methods of hacking (basically some basic types of attack also common which we have already disused in chapter-2 "Ways of hacking"). Here the 'white hat hackers' plays important role to help them to protect the companies/organizations/business from these hackers and we know that with the time the need of 'white hat hacker' is also increases.

In the cyber security filed you did not need any particular type of certification or degree for their work but if you have degree or certification of white hat it also help to grow in your field after a while we will discuss how can you get certification as 'white hat hacker' and anyone can get work in these filed if you have talent or skills and if you want make carrier in this field and it is one the best paying job in the field f cyber security and it is also good for those people who interested in learning something new.

If you are finding any job in the field of internet or technology or if you are belonging to engineering filed then it may also help you to get better jobs and new opportunities.

There we understand that the need of white hat hacker is also increase with time and it is new opportunities for the people in this filed. But in hacking always choose white hat hacking because it is legal.

- ## Certification of white hat hacker-

Basically in the field of cyber security you can did not need any proper certification for job because the work of white hat hacker depends upon their skills and how he/she protect the companies from their skills and many reputed hacker worldwide did not have certification but they are in good position so if you have skills then basis of your skills you will get paid in this filed. But it did not mean certification is nothing in this filed many organizations hire people according to their certification.

Certification-

The world wide most reputed organization named as **EC COUNCIL** it is most popular organization who conduct examination for the white hat hacker and complete details about the examination or certification and there criteria is available on their website and syllabus of examination is also on their website.

Chapter-4 completed

I HOPE YOU LEARN SOMETHING NEW SO NOW IT'S TIME TO GO ON OUR NEW CHAPTER.

PROTECTION AGAINST SOCIAL ATTACK

Introduction of chapter-

In this chapter we are going to understand of the important thing in the cyber security and it is one of the important topics.

What we are going to understand

1. Protection against phishing
2. Spyware or malware attack
3. Carding
4. Key logger
5. Usb hacking
6. Email spam and urgency account span
7. Distribution between real and fake web website.
8. Benefits of anti-virus and how to use it properly

1. Protection against phishing

It is one of the most popular ways to hack and mostly hackers use this in different types to hack the victim. In chapter-2 we have already discuss how phishing attack are performed by the hacker. Here we are going to understand how you can protect your personal and important data from this hacker.

The hacker have different ways to sends you on this website like throw emails(mainly) or throw web and many other ways. In this topic we basically deals with how hacker hack your data throw email Because email is one of the most popular way to take you on this website.
By any mean hackers wants to take you on these fake website or pages by any methods basically hacker use some common way to influence you to on this websites like as by mail, promotional offer or discount or throw website.

To protect yourself from phishing from mail then follow given points below-

- Don't click or open those mails which are in spam folder of your email box because Google or other email providing company review this mail from last history. And sometimes throw these mail some additional file is also attach of malwares (we will discuss more about in this chapter)
- Check the mail id of the sender(hacker easily bypass this)
- Compare that mail with other mail of particular company or organization
- Check the word mistake or grammar mistake (because in the reputed companies mail we may did not seen any mistakes of word or grammar
- If you think these entire thing are correct and when you click on the website first **check the URL of the website.**

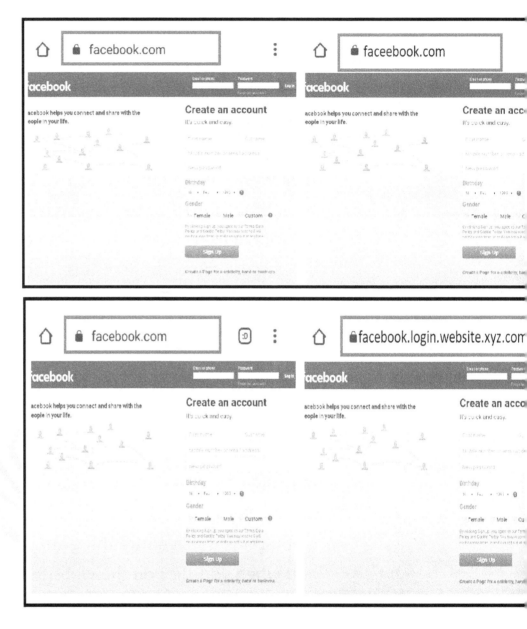

Note- sometimes some mails of the spam box are not spamming they are just mistakenly added in the spam email box.

To protect you from phishing from web or any other source then follow given points below-

- First check the security of the website like(https)
- Then check the URL of the website.
  Let's take an example for better understanding-
  E.g. 1 -The hacker buy related domain of original website like **faceebook.com** or **faceboook.**com now you are thinking everything is book but now check the spelling of the website (**original website-facebook.com**) in first one's" is extra and second having "O" extra and you may thing It is ok and you ignore this but this is fake phishing which is created to hack you (to

protect users from these different domain related to original website the owner of the website also buy some related domain but something these are already register and hacker or the owner these website sometime misuse them.)

E.g. 2- you many have sometimes seen that many big companies use there sub. Domain like as login.google.com but the hacker also misuse them they buy domain or makes domain like **login.facebook.xyz.com** but the people might think it is real and spelling of facebook is also correct by here the hacker use sub domain in different way **so to protect them self also check complete url before .com, .in, .xyz, web etc**.

Note – It educational purposes or for self protection so did not use them for illegal purpose and here my intension is also to educate people among hacking and how to protect themselves from it.

- **Here we learn how can you protect yourself from some phishing attack now we are going to learn how can you protect yourself from spyware and malware.**

2. Spyware or malware attack-

If you are using the system of any organization ,company ,business where the data of the company is stored or connected to company server where all personal information of the company is stored them also avoid to download unwanted data from unauthorized website (something the malware also downloaded throw repute website and repute software) throw internet In your system and always try to download data from "reputed websites" and always use good antivirus to protect because some malware will install in your computer by any mean because they are very small and bind to other software or files of your system.

If you are using your personal computer then also try to avoid downloading of unwanted software from unauthorized website and always use anti-virus.

A Note- Basic step of protection is same for all. The biggest mistake mostly people do –

After installing anti-virus the mostly people didn't update the anti-virus, it lead to create to create a low pole for the system so the new malware which are new for the anti-virus the antivirus did not detect them because thousands of new malware are created daily and the anti-virus companies update their anti-virus to fight against malware they update them time to time but many the people did not install latest version of anti-virus so it lead a passage for the malware and the anti-virus did not work as barrier between system and the malware. So to protect your system from virus you need to update your anti-virus so it can work more efficiency and helps you to keep your data safe.

Now we know how you can protect your system from malwares.

Spyware- it is unit of malware or part of malware but it is very small ant many anti-virus cannot detect them and this spyware or malware are mostly download from those website when are either illegal or having pirated content and throw many porn website because in the world of internet the system or internet is very smart and many people run java script on their website so many applications are downloaded in your system without your permission and bind to other software and the anti-virus can't detect them and even you did not know your system is hacking.

Some common methods to check if your system is hacked or not-

i. If you system is slow below normal from sometimes because malware duplicate very fast in the system and it takes more memory from your system and due to which your system will become slow because they did not getting proper memory for their function.

ii. If your system are consuming more battery then normal from sometimes when you connect throw internet it happens because malware start there functions and sending data to their owner.

Note- sometimes your system may be slow or consume more battery because sometime companies slow there old devices when they are launching new version of the system or something it is happen due to when you are using more applications or using high processing software in low capacity device.

iii. Those devices which are affect by malware it create unwanted ads on your system screen.(something it is happen due to internal software of the system which is by default installed by the brand of the system.

iv. We the system consume more internet either when you are not serving anything then it may be due to the malware sending or uploading your data to the server (but it doesn't mean those computer which are not infected by the malware did not consume internet because some applications consume internet in the background).

3. Carding

Basically carding is another why of hacking where hacker hack your bank card details by different methods and how can you protect yourself-
 Definition-Carding is nothing just a way of get the credit card details of the victims by different methods
Lets now understand the mechanism of carding -

a. When you buy a service or a product throw internet and pay money throw your credit card which is issued by your bank and when you enter your card details on this website the website store your data on there server for future payment now suppose the website will hacked them your card details which are stored on the website server are now in the control of hacker and now hacker can use your card for future payments which gives you a great loss of money.

b. The hacker can create a website or throw marking offering you a discount a takes you on their website and when you enter you card details for the payment the hacker can get excess your card and it can transfer or you your money for personal use and it also gives a great loss of money to you.

c. In the above two ways hacker hack your card details throw internet but one more may of carding may be possible. Let's suppose you are buying something throw supermarket near your house and you are paying money throw your card. When you swipe your card in there machine for the payment. Here the machine can store your card details and it also get your pin when you enter and now the super market owner or hacker use your card and gives you a great loss of money.

Here we understand how carding is perform now we will understand how can you protect yourself from it-
Online-

If you are paying money online throw your card also check the website is real or not and also check the security of the website (e.g. check https) or also prefer https because it is more secure then http website. Here https website gives you extra protection against hacking.

Always done payment on that website which is reputed in the market place and secure and avoid the websites which are giving you lot of discount because mostly these website are fake and they just hack your card details and your other personal data.

Here I am not talking about the entire website. If a reputed website giving you this type of discount then you can use this website for payment because they are genuine and highly secure (with some exception).

Note- when you will know that your account has been hacked or someone is using your card details without your permission then as soon as possible inform to your respective bank or your issued credit card company and block your card temporary.

4. Key logger

We have already disused about key logger and its types.

Key logger- two types

   a. Software key logger
   b. Physical or hardware key logger

   Now it's time to understand each of them-

   a. Software key logger-

   As we already know a software is installed in our system and saves all the Command done by the help our keyboard. To protect yourself from hacking always try to use own computer for personal uses like for your bank account or social media account and you already know that some key logger are also install throw internet and sends data to their owner to protect from this you can us you can use good anti-virus to protect.

b. Physical or hardware key logger-

We already know that physical or hardware key logger is mostly present in public computer where the different people use these computer to excess there account. It is mostly seen in cyber café computer and the owner of the cyber café can excess your information which you enter throw your keyboard like email, bank details , social media account password or other data, if you ever seen physical key logger in cyber café computer you can complain in cyber branch of police and the police will help you and file case against cyber café owner why cyber café owner use these physical key logger if the owner can't explain then they will be jailed for the use of physical key logger and to use people account without their permission.

Uses/ benefits of key logger like as-

1. The key logger can be used by the parents to monitor the online activities

of their children and protect their children if he/she doing anything wrong on internet.

2. The key logger may be useful for the organization because the owner of the logger can monitor the working activity of their employees and monitor if the employees were anything wrong or doing work against the organization or companies.

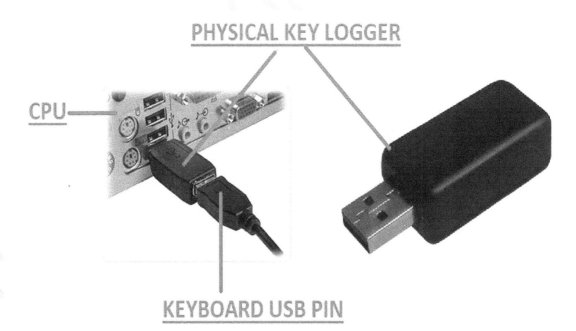

PHYSICAL KEY LOGGER

CPU

KEYBOARD USB PIN

5. Usb hacking

You might many time listen that don't use any other people pen drive because the virus may be present in the pen drive of that people then that virus may also transmit to our system because many malware duplicate very rapidly and when you insert that malware infected pen drive the malware which attached to the files of that pen drive also enter in your system and bind with your files and due to duplication of malware it will infect your complete computer and the hacker get excess to your computer due to which your system will consume more memory of your system due to which your system will become slow and when the computer connect to internet the malware sends all the data to their owner and due to which the system will consume more battery then normal and system will consume more internet then normal or before malware attack and most important all the data of your system is now in the control under the hacker.

Some malware are also present in new pen drive so always buy pen drive of big brands and before uploading data in pen drive first format them so the malware will not affect your system.

Protection-

To protect from usb hacking did not use unwanted pen drive and before accessing the pen drive always scan then with good anti-virus so the changes of protection against usb hacking increases. It is the easiest way of protection against usb hacking.

6. Email spam and urgency account span-

It is same as phishing where the hacker sends you mail and create urgency you to excess your account like as it may sends you have not using your account from many time or your account has been hacked or the company update their policy by these method or any other method they can create urgency and you will thing it is original mail from the company because it is look same as official mail of the website and when you click on the given link to excess the website you will redirected to fake website which is created by the hacker and when you enter your personal details and click on login button all the details where store in hacker's server and now hacker get the excess of your account now the hacker use your account for their own benefits.

How to protect from it-

- The company never sends you these types of mail.
- If you get this type of mail always contact to your companies regarding the mail.
- After clicking the URL check the URL of the website.

    These are the some basic ways so you can protect from cyber attacks.

7. Distribution between real and fake website

We have already discussed majority of the distribution between real and fake web page now here we are going to understand more about this topic-

Let's take an example for better understanding-

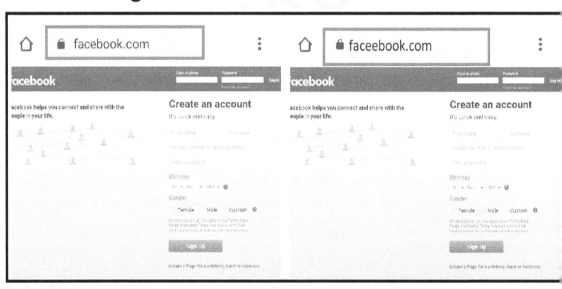

In the above image we are using two pages one of them is real and other one is fake.
In the first check the URL of the website which is facebook.com and other one is faceebook.com are you find any difference between them.

No, now again see the URL and check the spelling of face book, have you find any difference between then,

 Yes, so by buying similar domain of related website the hacker hack your personal data and we already discussed how the hacker take you on these website.

e.g. 2

Here the second example for more better understand

Before understanding the above image lets understand some basic things related to web designing and domain.

Many time you have seen that many big companies e.g. google.com use their sub domain for their website like as youtube.google.com here the google.com is the main domain and here the word YouTube work as sub-domain.

So let's understand how hackers use this for hacking-

Those people who know basic about of hacking they did not fall in first way of phishing so hacker started using one another may like as they make sub domain for their website like show in the above image as login.facebook.xyz.com so when people see the url they might thing everything is ok but this type of pages are fake and created by the hacker for their personal gain.

So now the question arise how to check the page is real or not.

a) Firstly check the security of the website (prefer –https secure website)

b) Then check the URL of website

There are two types of error

1. Check the spelling of the domain which we discuss in example-1 if you find any mistake in the spelling of the website then it is fake website and copy from original website to gain your information.

2. Check complete URL which we disused in example-2 if you find that the sub domain or domain is not of original website and it is created to gain/hack your information by the hacker.

9. **Benefits of anti-virus and how to use it properly-**
A good anti-virus may protect you from many malwares spyware and it gives you and additional sheet of protection from malware attack and helps you to keep your data safe but many types the malware will infect your system in the presence by anti-virus this is happen due to when people not update their anti-virus or the anti-virus company did not update their anti-virus to protect against new

malware attack. So always try to keep your system from updated anti-virus which not 100 % protect you but it protect you in many ways and it helps to keep your data personal.

CHAPTER-5 COMPLETED
I HOPE YOU LEARN SOMETHING NEW.

All the content provided in this book are only for educational purposes and for self protection and all the information in this book are from internet search and from my knowledge and I tried my best to provide best information and I am not responsible for any error in this book and I am not taking any legal information.